The Federal Bureau of Investigation's Sentinel Program

The FBI implemented Sentinel in July 2012 as an electronic information and case management system that includes records management, workflow management, evidence management, search and reporting capabilities, and information sharing with other law enforcement agencies and the intelligence community. Development of Sentinel first began in 2006 and at the time it was expected to be completed in December 2009 at a cost of $425 million. This report, the Department of Justice Office of the Inspector General's tenth report on Sentinel, examines Sentinel's effect on the FBI's daily operations while also reviewing Sentinel's project costs and the updates made to the program since it was deployed.[1]

This report focuses on users' experiences with Sentinel's functionality and their ability to effectively and efficiently enter, search, and share information in the FBI's case management system. To accomplish this audit, we surveyed and interviewed Sentinel users to assess user satisfaction with the system, examined Sentinel's budget and incurred costs, and reviewed the improvements that were made to or planned for Sentinel as of July 2014.

Our review found that most FBI employees routinely used Sentinel to perform their daily investigative activities. The majority of FBI employees responding to our survey reported that Sentinel has had an overall positive impact on the FBI's operations, making the FBI better able to carry out its mission, and better able to share information. The majority of survey respondents also reported that Sentinel had a positive impact on the FBI's efficiency, by allowing improvements such as reducing the number of lost documents, decreasing the amount of time that it takes to get documents approved and improving the FBI's ability to share documents within the FBI.

Sentinel users did, however, express dissatisfaction with two major functions of Sentinel: search and indexing. Sentinel's search function provides users the capability to locate cases and specific case-related information within Sentinel. According to a July 2012 FBI report, the search function is both flexible and powerful enough to accommodate the substantial volume and wide variety of information available for retrieval in Sentinel.[2] Yet we found that only 42 percent of

---

[1] The previous report assessed a July 2012 status report prepared by the FBI and submitted by the Department of Justice in response a congressional directive. Appendix III contains a list of prior OIG Sentinel reports.

[2] U.S. Department of Justice, *Congressional Report on The Federal Bureau of Investigation's Next Generation Information and Case Management Program* (July 2012). Although submitted by the Department of Justice, the FBI prepared the report.

the respondents to our survey who used Sentinel's search functionality often received the results they needed. In the comment section of our survey, 20 respondents also specifically stated that the search function in the Automated Case Support system (ACS), the FBI's prior case management system, was superior to the search function in Sentinel.[3] Twenty-three respondents also reported that Sentinel returned either too many search results for users to reasonably review or no results at all for a document the user knew existed. In response to our finding regarding the search function, the Sentinel Program Manager told us that the FBI recognized the need to improve Sentinel's search function and provided documentation to show that updates were made to improve the search function. We have not assessed the impact of these updates on the user experience. The FBI also told us that some of the user's concerns will be addressed with the deployment of Sentinel 1.5.

The purpose of the indexing function is to designate, modify, and delete the relationship between any two identifiers, such as the relationship between a person and that person's address.[4] Based upon our fieldwork and survey results, we also found that users' primary concern with Sentinel's indexing function was the amount of administrative burden placed on the author of a document because the author is also responsible for indexing the document. For example, 41 percent of survey respondents reported that they spent more time indexing in Sentinel than they did in ACS, the system that Sentinel replaced. One small subset of respondents - Evidence Custodian Technicians and Electronic Surveillance Technicians expressed concerns that Sentinel decreased their daily productivity by increasing the time spent storing and managing evidence collected by the FBI. Similarly, a majority of the Special Agents we surveyed reported that Sentinel decreased their daily productivity and attributed the decrease to an increase in the administrative burden posed by indexing, which has left them with less time for investigative activities. We also found that Operational Support Technicians (OST), who played a significant role in the indexing process prior to Sentinel's deployment, were not always used efficiently or assigned new tasks to replace their previous duties. Although the FBI told us that they previously provided training to OST supervisors, to better manage their OST staff, survey responses indicate concerns with the utilization of OSTs. As a result, we believe that some user concerns, especially those surrounding indexing, may require both a technical and business process solution.

Survey respondents also reported that Sentinel was missing features that they believed are critical to their duties, including features related to Sentinel's integration with other FBI information technology systems. We also found that although respondents were generally satisfied with the job-specific training and other resources the FBI offered, Special Agents and Supervisory Special Agents

---

[3] Implemented in October 1995, ACS was the FBI's case management system until July 2012.

[4] The identifiers that can be indexed include persons, organizations, locations, incidents, property, and communication accounts.

reported a significant decline in their level of satisfaction with the availability of technical and policy-related support after the deployment of Sentinel.

Our review also found that the total budget for Sentinel since the deployment of Sentinel 1.0 in July 2012 has increased from $451 million to $551.4 million. This increase is the result of operations and maintenance during FY 2013 and 2014 and the development of new functionality during FY 2014. As of July 2014, the FBI had obligated $529.2 million of that $551.4 million and expensed $502.1 million.[5]

Since the July 2012 initial release of Sentinel 1.0, the FBI has made four significant updates to the system, all of which were associated with operations and maintenance activities. Following the deployment of Sentinel 1.4 in September 2013, the FBI began work on its fifth significant update, Sentinel 1.5, which is scheduled to be deployed in October 2014. Sentinel 1.5 is intended to support the needs of the FBI's intelligence analysts by integrating legacy intelligence systems and expanding Sentinel's functionality by leveraging its features to support the FBI's intelligence mission.

As part of our audit follow-up process, we also assessed the FBI's efforts to implement corrective actions in response to our prior recommendations and determined that all of these recommendations have been adequately addressed.

This report contains three new recommendations to the FBI to help ensure that the FBI's business processes are aligned with Sentinel's design and functionalities, and that Sentinel's search and index functions efficiently meet the needs of FBI employees.

---

[5] The FBI has reported that, as of July 2014, it had obligated $432 million of the $451 million available for Sentinel in FY 2012 at the time Sentinel 1.0 was deployed. However, as discussed in our December 2011 and September 2012 reports, these obligated and budgeted amounts did not include costs for 2 years of operations and maintenance after Sentinel was completed, costs that were part of the $451 million cost estimate that the FBI projected for Sentinel in 2008.

AUDIT OF THE STATUS OF THE FEDERAL BUREAU OF INVESTIGATION'S SENTINEL PROGRAM

TABLE OF CONTENTS

INTRODUCTION 1

    Background 1

    Sentinel 1.0 Major Functional Areas... 2

    Office of the Inspector General Audit Approach 4

FINDINGS AND RECOMMENDATIONS 6

SENTINEL PROGRAM STATUS... 6

    User Observations on Sentinel Functionality 6

    Sentinel Budget.. 21

    Sentinel Enhancements 21

    Conclusion... 23

    Recommendations 24

STATEMENT ON INTERNAL CONTROLS 25

STATEMENT ON COMPLIANCE WITH LAWS AND REGULATIONS 26

APPENDIX I - OBJECTIVE, SCOPE, AND METHODOLOGY........................ 27

    Objectives 27

    Scope and Methodology... 27

**APPENDIX II- RESULTS OF ALL SENTINEL SURVEYS EXCLUDING
RESPONDENTS' BACKGROUND QUESTIONS** 30

**APPENDIX III - OFFICE OF THE INSPECTOR GENERAL
SENTINEL REPORTS**..37

**APPENDIX IV – FEDERAL BUREAU OF INVESTIGATION RESPONSE TO
THE DRAFT AUDIT REPORT** 38

**APPENDIX V - OFFICE OF THE INSPECTOR GENERAL ANALYSIS AND
SUMMARY OF ACTIONS NECESSARY TO CLOSE THE REPORT**...................40

THE FEDERAL BUREAU OF INVESTIGATION'S
SENTINEL PROGRAM

INTRODUCTION

This is the tenth in a series of reports by the Department of Justice Office of the Inspector General (OIG) examining Sentinel, the Federal Bureau of Investigation's (FBI) information and investigative case management system.

In our prior report, released in September 2012, we assessed a Department of Justice (Department) July 2012 status report on the Sentinel program that was prepared in response to a congressional directive.[6] We found that the estimated cost of $441 million to complete Sentinel implementation did not include costs for 2 years of operations and maintenance (O&M) after Sentinel was completed. These costs were part of the original projected cost of $451 million for Sentinel in 2008. In addition, we found that the FBI continued to operate other information technology (IT) systems that were supposed to be subsumed by Sentinel because the FBI decided to not include certain functionality originally intended for Sentinel. Although data provided by the FBI indicated that FBI employees were routinely using Sentinel to perform their daily electronic workflow and investigative activities, we were unable to confirm that the FBI had completed 15 of 17 key development milestones listed in the schedule estimate contained in the July 2012 report.

Background

The FBI's attempt to move from a paper-based record system to an electronic case management system began in 2001 with the Virtual Case File, a major component of the FBI's Trilogy IT modernization project. The FBI abandoned the Virtual Case File project in 2005 after spending $170 million, and subsequently announced the award of a $305 million contract to Lockheed Martin as part of a project to develop Sentinel, a new electronic case management system. At the time, the FBI estimated that the total cost of Sentinel would be $425 million.

---

[6] The Conference Report accompanying Public Law 112-55 (enacted on November 18, 2011) directed the Attorney General to provide a status report to the committees within 120 days of enactment of the Act and to submit the report to the OIG at the same time for our review. The Conference Report also directed the OIG to provide an assessment of the Department's report to the Committees on Appropriations within 60 days of receiving the Department's report.

The Department provided its report – *Congressional Report on the Federal Bureau of Investigation's Next Generation Information and Case Management Program*, July 3, 2012 – to the Committees and to the OIG on July 9, 2012.

The OIG provided its report – *Interim Report on the Federal Bureau of Investigation's Implementation Status of the Federal Bureau of Investigation's Implementation of the Sentinel Project*, Report 12-38 – to the Committees on September 7, 2012.

In addition to being an official FBI records repository, Sentinel was intended to be a user-friendly, web-based electronic case management system that would give FBI agents and analysts the ability to manage evidence and automate the document review and approval process. The FBI planned to migrate all data from the Automated Case Support system (ACS) to Sentinel and eventually retire ACS.[7]

In June 2007, the FBI announced that it had fully deployed Phase 1 of Sentinel, which delivered a web-based portal to ACS and workboxes for FBI agents and supervisors that summarized case information.[8]

In June 2010, an independent assessment projected it would take the FBI an additional 6 years and $351 million to finish Sentinel.[9] In October 2010, the FBI assumed from Lockheed Martin direct control of, and responsibility for, Sentinel development activities and initiated an Agile approach to developing Sentinel.[10] After extending its scheduled deployment 6 months, the FBI deployed a fully functional Sentinel system, Sentinel 1.0, in July 2012. Since deploying Sentinel 1.0, the FBI has updated Sentinel to address routine defects that were discovered after its deployment and to improve its performance and provide minor enhancements to its functionality.[11]

Sentinel 1.0 Major Functional Areas

In a July 2012 report to Congress, the Department stated that Sentinel satisfied 14 major functional areas, including case management, collected items management, indexing, records management, search, work item authoring and

---

[7] Implemented in October 1995, ACS, which the FBI has not yet retired, was the FBI's case management system until July 2012. As of May 2011, ACS contained records for over 9.4 million cases. While ACS is an electronic repository of investigative documents, it does not have the capability for FBI employees to electronically sign documents. As a result, when ACS was the FBI's case management system, FBI agents and officials had to sign printed copies of the documents contained in ACS. These printed copies of investigative documents are the official records.

[8] A personal workbox summarizes a user's cases and leads. A lead is a request from an FBI field office or a headquarters division for assistance in an investigation. A squad workbox helps supervisors manage personnel resources.

[9] The independent assessment was performed by Mitre, a federally funded research and development center that assists the government with scientific research and analysis; development and acquisition of large, complex systems; and systems engineering and integration.

[10] The Agile development approach to software development focuses on the frequent delivery of capabilities through the close collaboration of users, developers, and testers. The Agile development approach seeks to deliver value to users quickly even in an environment where the requirements and technology are frequently changing.

[11] Sentinel 1.1, 1.2, 1.3, and 1.4 are updated versions of Sentinel that were deployed based on enhancements or O&M activities. Sentinel 1.1 was released in September 2012 and Sentinel 1.4 was released in September 2013.

work flow.[12] A summary of selected Sentinel functional areas is presented in Table 1 below.

TABLE 1: SUMMARY OF SELECTED SENTINEL FUNCTIONAL AREAS

Sentinel Functional Area	Functional Task or Ability
Case Management	Oversight of the investigative and administrative activities associated with a case.
Collected Items Management	Activities associated with documenting the collection, storage, and tracking of physical items related to FBI cases.
Indexing	Collection and maintenance of investigative and administrative information about persons, organizations, locations, incidents, property, and communication accounts.[13]
Records Management	Functions required to manage the records entered in to official FBI case files.
Search	Ability to locate different types of information connected within Sentinel.
Work Item Authoring	Memorialization of the work that has been accomplished or is in the process of being accomplished and association of that work with specific cases.
Work Flow	Integrated tools that allow FBI personnel to create, read, update, and delete documents and other work items. Also allows users to author or co-author work items.[14]

Source: OIG Analysis of the Department's July 2012 Report to Congress

As we discussed in our September 2012 report on Sentinel, there were additions, modifications, or deletions to the requirements for each of the 14 major functional areas. Requirements for various functional areas were deleted because

---

[12] U.S. Department of Justice, *Congressional Report on The Federal Bureau of Investigation's Next Generation Information and Case Management Program* (July 2012).

[13] Indexing allows Sentinel to add structure to the data it contains, which in turn enables improved search results. As the FBI noted in a document that describes the index feature to its employees, a search for white males who drive black cars using a search engine like those used for internet searches would return all documents that mention any of the following: white males, black males, white cars, or black cars. By adding structure to the data through indexing, Sentinel's search function is able to return only white males who drive a black car. When a user indexes an entity, the system will suggest potential matches already indexed in Sentinel.

[14] U.S. Department of Justice, *Congressional Report on The Federal Bureau of Investigation's Next Generation Information and Case Management Program* (July 2012).

the capability described in those requirements was met by other systems. For example, the Case Management and Work Item Authoring functional areas had a significant percentage of deleted requirements, 17 percent and 22 percent, respectively. The Interface functional area had the largest percentage of added requirements, 86 percent. We also found in our September 2012 report that some of the requirements had been transferred to other FBI IT systems, including Delta and iData.[15] Six requirements were deleted because Delta subsumed two legacy human intelligence systems originally planned to be subsumed by Sentinel. As described below, we found in the current audit that the FBI is continuing to improve Sentinel and the forthcoming version 1.5 will be the first major functional enhancement since Sentinel's initial deployment in July 2012.[16]

Office of the Inspector General Audit Approach

The OIG conducted this audit to assess Sentinel's functionality, its impact on the FBI's efficiency, and the FBI's ability to share information. We also examined Sentinel program costs incurred and budgeted, and system improvements completed and planned since Sentinel was deployed. We interviewed Sentinel users and conducted a survey designed to gather information about system deployment, system usage, ease of use, the quality of training, and whether Sentinel users were satisfied with Sentinel and viewed it as an improvement over ACS. We sent the survey to 2,513 FBI employees and we received 1,150 responses to the survey.

To optimize and customize our surveys for the appropriate audiences, we interviewed Special Agents, Supervisory Special Agents, Operational Support Technicians (OST), Support Services Technicians (SST), Intelligence Analysts, Electronic Surveillance (ELSUR) Technicians and Evidence Custodian Technicians (ECT), and other personnel in field offices and FBI headquarters. Because Sentinel users with different job titles require different functions of Sentinel, we deployed four different versions of our survey according to job title: (1) Special Agents; (2) Supervisory Special Agents; (3) ECTs, ELSUR Technicians, and Operational Support Technicians; and (4) All Other Positions.[17] In addition, to track further enhancements and developments on Sentinel, we interviewed the Sentinel Project Manager and Chief Technology Officer, the Chief Information Officer, Sentinel Lead Developer, the Information Technology Engineering Division Assistant Director, and additional Special Agents. Finally, we reviewed Executive Steering Committee minutes and the release notes for each build of Sentinel.

---

[15] Delta is the FBI's confidential human source management system and iData is the Intelligence Data Association and Tagging application.

[16] Sentinel 1.5 is a development effort to add functionality to Sentinel that will support the specific needs of the FBI's Intelligence Analysts. Development of Sentinel 1.5 began in October 2013 and is scheduled to be deployed in October 2014.

[17] For the All Other Positions survey, respondents were asked to identity their job titles. The Intelligence Analyst position represented 28 percent of the participants who completed the All Other Positions survey.

As part of our audit follow-up process, we also assessed the FBI's efforts to implement corrective actions in response to our prior recommendations and determined that all of these recommendations have been adequately addressed. Appendix I contains a more detailed description of our audit objectives, scope, and methodology.

FINDINGS AND RECOMMENDATIONS

SENTINEL PROGRAM STATUS

In determining whether Sentinel users were satisfied with Sentinel and viewed it as an improvement over ACS, we found that the majority of survey respondents reported that overall Sentinel has had a positive impact on the FBI's operations, making the FBI more productive, better able to carry out its mission, and share information. However, interviews with Sentinel users and responses to detailed survey questions revealed Sentinel users' dissatisfaction with its search and indexing features, two major functions of Sentinel. Regarding search, we found that only 42 percent of the respondents to our survey who used Sentinel's search functionality often received the results they needed. In response to our finding regarding the search function, the Sentinel Program Manager told us that the FBI recognized the need to improve Sentinel's search function and provided documentation to show that updates were made to improve the search function. The FBI also told us that some of the user's concerns will be addressed with the deployment of Sentinel 1.5. Special Agents reported that the increase in the administrative burden associated with indexing leaves less time for investigative activities. In addition, 67 percent of ECTs and ELSUR Technicians survey respondents said that Sentinel had a negative impact on their daily productivity. For example, in interviews, ECTs expressed concerns regarding the increased amount of time it takes to charge evidence in and out of Evidence Control Rooms using Sentinel.

Since the deployment of Sentinel in July 2012, as a result of operations and maintenance (O&M) costs and the development of new functionality, the total budget for Sentinel increased from $451 million to $551.4 million. As of July 2014, the FBI had obligated $529.2 million of that amount. Since Sentinel's deployment in July 2012, the FBI has released periodic system updates. In addition, in October 2013, the FBI began developing the first new functional area since Sentinel was initially deployed. This and other enhancements to Sentinel, which are intended to provide new functionality for the FBI's intelligence analysts by integrating other IT systems and enhancing system interfaces, are scheduled to be deployed with Sentinel 1.5 in October 2014.

User Observations on Sentinel Functionality

In order to assess Sentinel's functionality, its impact on the FBI's efficiency, and the FBI's ability to share information, we conducted interviews and surveyed 2,513 Sentinel users. Our survey was designed to determine whether Sentinel provides FBI agents and analysts with the ability to author and review case documents using an electronic workflow, provide users with the search results they need to link cases with similar information, and effectively and efficiently manage evidence. The survey addressed major components of Sentinel's functionality including its user friendliness, case management, evidence management, information sharing, and automated review and approval process.[18]

Our user survey indicated that, overall, Sentinel has increased the daily productivity of FBI employees, enhanced the FBI's ability to carry out its mission, and increased their ability to share information with colleagues not located in their office. We also reviewed narrative survey responses and found that survey respondents provided positive feedback on Sentinel's ability to upload, send, view, and store documentation. In addition, survey respondents noted that Sentinel has made it easier to collaborate on routine documents and track the status of work products and communications. Some survey respondents also stated that Sentinel is an improvement over ACS.

Through responses to specific survey questions and the additional narrative responses, users also expressed dissatisfaction with the indexing and search functions in Sentinel. One small subset of respondents – ECTs and ELSUR Technicians – responded negatively about a range of topics including Sentinel's impact on their productivity and the Sentinel training they received.[19] Survey respondents' narrative responses expressed concerns with the transfer of administrative responsibilities from OSTs to Special Agents and integrating Sentinel with other systems. These results are described in more detail below.

Broad Measures of Sentinel's Impact

The user survey respondents were asked several questions related to their overall experience using the Sentinel system. These questions addressed:

- Survey respondents' overall satisfaction with the FBI's handling of the transition from ACS to Sentinel,

- Sentinel's impact on respondents' daily productivity,

- Sentinel's impact on sharing information outside of their office, and

- Sentinel's impact on the FBI's ability to carry out its mission.

The majority of survey respondents, 63 percent, were satisfied with the FBI's handling of the transition from ACS to Sentinel. Likewise, 58 percent of

---

[18] Detailed results of our survey are contained in Appendix II.

[19] ECTs are responsible for the receipt, retention and disposition of evidence for the field office. ELSUR Technicians maintain ELSUR physical evidence and ensures chain of custody is preserved.

respondents reported that Sentinel has increased their daily productivity. In addition, 69 percent of respondents reported that Sentinel increased their ability to share information with personnel in other offices, and 72 percent of survey respondents indicated that Sentinel has enhanced the FBI's ability to carry out its mission.

ECTs and ELSUR Technicians represented only 3 percent of the total number of survey respondents but, due to the nature of their positions, they rely heavily on Sentinel to complete their work — 71 percent of ECTs and ELSUR Technicians reported spending more than 30 hours per week working in Sentinel. As shown in the following exhibit, ECTs and ELSUR Technicians survey respondents viewed Sentinel's impact on their productivity much more negatively than survey respondents in other job positions.

EXHIBIT 1: SENTINEL EFFECT ON PRODUCTIVITY BY JOB TITLE[20]

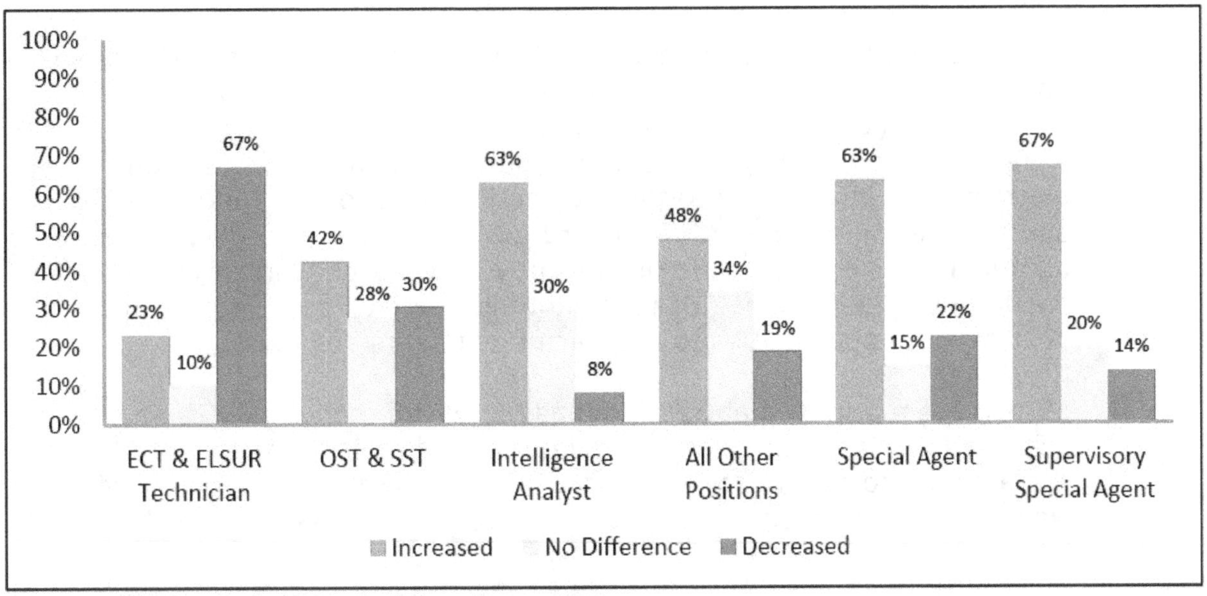

Source: OIG Analysis of Sentinel User Survey Data

During our fieldwork interviews, ECTs expressed concerns with how Sentinel affected their daily work, such as charging evidence in and out of Evidence Control Rooms and other approved storage locations, inventory of evidence, recordkeeping of evidence, and concerns with the time recorded for transfer of evidence in the chain of custody. ECTs also told us that they had to maintain two chains of custody for each piece of evidence, a paper chain of custody and a chain of custody in Sentinel. Pursuant to FBI policy, the paper chain of custody is the official record; however, ECTs are also responsible for ensuring that the same information is recorded accurately in Sentinel. They said they found this process duplicative and

---

[20] Due to rounding, the sum of the percentages in some of this report's exhibits does not equal 100 percent.

inefficient, and they told us it can be difficult to ensure both records contain the same information. The FBI told us that the electronic chain of custody in Sentinel is used as a backup in the event the paper chain of custody is lost or destroyed. If this situation were to occur, the FBI would be able to recreate an accurate chain of custody based upon the information retained in Sentinel.

Sentinel Impact on Operational Efficiency

As an electronic case management system, Sentinel was designed to improve the effectiveness and efficiency of the FBI's day-to-day operations. We asked Sentinel users whether they believed the current processes in place since Sentinel's implementation had improved operational efficiency compared to ACS and the FBI's previous paper-based processes. We analyzed user responses and found that the majority of survey respondents believe that the Sentinel processes are an improvement over the previous processes.[21] For example, among users who responded to the following survey questions:

- 57 percent reported a reduction in misplaced documentation. Because paper documents were the official record under ACS, documents were physically circulated for approval and filing, and some of these documents were misplaced; with Sentinel, many documents are now handled electronically instead. According to the FBI, due to legal and financial audit requirements the official record for some documents continues to be on paper. For example, the official copy of a search warrant is a paper document. Because the FBI could not eliminate all paper forms and documents, opportunities to misplace documents still exist.

- 69 percent reported that Sentinel has increased their ability to share information with colleagues located outside of their office.[22] In ACS, only the author and supervisor were able to review a paper document before it was approved and signed, which often took days, delaying the sharing of information.

- 53 percent of Special Agents reported they spent less time drafting an FD-302, which the FBI uses to record investigative activity, such as the results of an interview.

- 60 percent of Special Agents reported they spent less time drafting electronic communications (ECs).

---

[21] As discussed previously in the OIG Audit Approach section of this report, Sentinel users with different job titles require different functions of Sentinel. As a result, we deployed four different versions of our survey according to job title: (1) Special Agents; (2) Supervisory Special Agents; (3) ECTs, ELSUR Technicians, and Operational Support Technicians; and (4) All Other Positions.

[22] This question was only presented to those users whose job positions require them to share information outside of their office.

- 59 percent reported a reduction in the time they spend approving forms.[23]

- 63 percent reported a reduction in the time they spend approving ECs.[24]

- 69 percent reported a reduction in the time it takes to get documents approved.[25] As described above, the process for approving documents in ACS relied on paper records. According to survey respondents, Sentinel's electronic workflow appears to have reduced the amount of time it takes to get documents approved.

In addition, as illustrated in Exhibit 2 below, over 70 percent of survey respondents reported that they found it easy to learn how to complete common Sentinel tasks such as drafting a form, approving a form, drafting an EC, or approving an EC.

---

[23] Only users in the Supervisory Special Agents and All Other Positions categories were asked this question because users in other job positions generally did not approve forms.

[24] Only users in the Supervisory Special Agents and All Other Positions categories were asked this question because users in other job positions generally did not approve ECs.

[25] Users in Special Agents, Operational Support Technicians, and All Other Positions categories were asked about the reduction in time to get documents approved.

EXHIBIT 2: EASE OF LEARNING TO DRAFT AND APPROVE FD-302, EC, AND OTHER FORMS

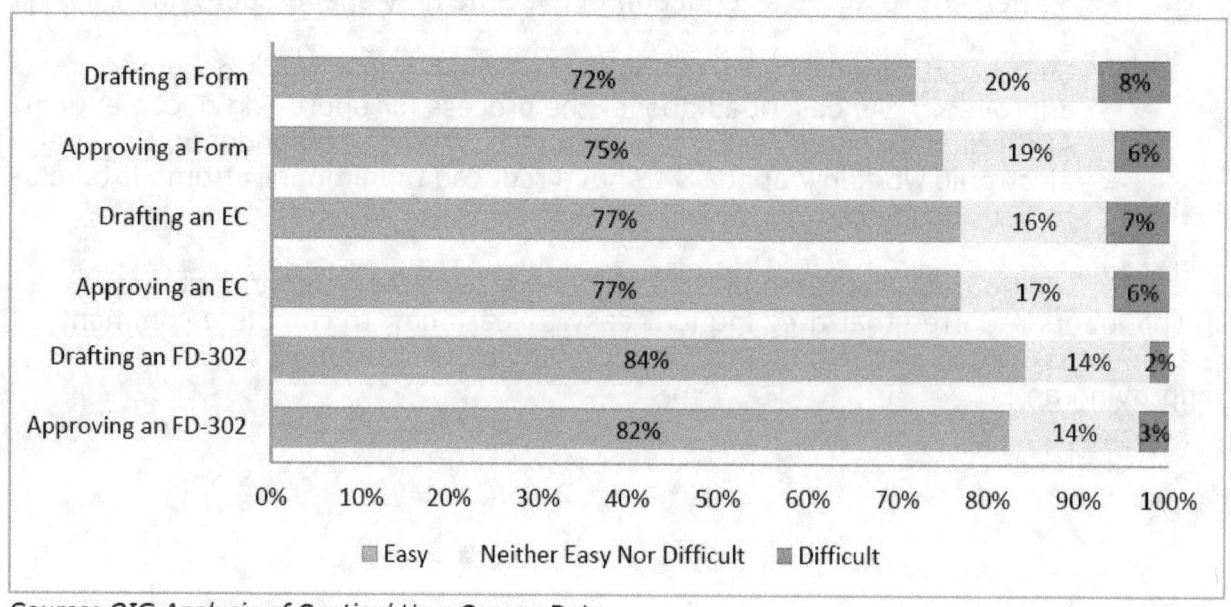

Source: OIG Analysis of Sentinel User Survey Data

Search and Indexing Functions

Users reported challenges learning how to use the search and indexing functions and in obtaining the results that they needed from the search function. Sentinel's search function provides users with the capability to locate cases and specific case-related information within Sentinel. For example, a Special Agent can search for bank robberies in a particular city or pictures related to a specific investigation. In broad terms, indexing is the collection and maintenance of investigative and administrative information about persons, organizations, locations, incidents, property, and communication accounts. Indexing allows Sentinel to add structure to the data it contains, which in turn enables improved search results.[26] As the FBI noted in a document that describes the index feature to its employees, a search for white males who drive black cars using a search engine like those used for Internet searches would return all documents that mention any of the following: white males, black males, white cars, or black cars. By adding structure to the data through indexing, Sentinel's search function is able to return only white males who drive a black car.

<u>Search</u>

The search function provides users with the capability to locate different types of information contained within Sentinel. According to the FBI, the search function is both flexible and powerful enough to accommodate the substantial volume and wide variety of information available for retrieval in Sentinel. In our

---

[26] The search function includes the ability to search both structured and unstructured data.

11

current audit, we found that 59 percent of survey respondents who used Sentinel's search functionality reported that they sometimes, rarely, or never received the results they needed. In the comment section of our survey, 20 respondents also specifically stated that the search function in ACS was superior to the search function in Sentinel. In addition, we found that survey respondents' satisfaction with search results varied according to the location of the respondent, and FBI headquarters was the only location where the majority of respondents reported that they often received the search results they needed. As shown in the following exhibit, a majority of survey respondents from FBI field offices, Legal Attachés (Legat), and Resident Agencies reported that search only sometimes, rarely, or never provided the results they needed.

EXHIBIT 3: FREQUENCY WITH WHICH SEARCH PROVIDED USERS WITH NEEDED RESULTS BY LOCATION

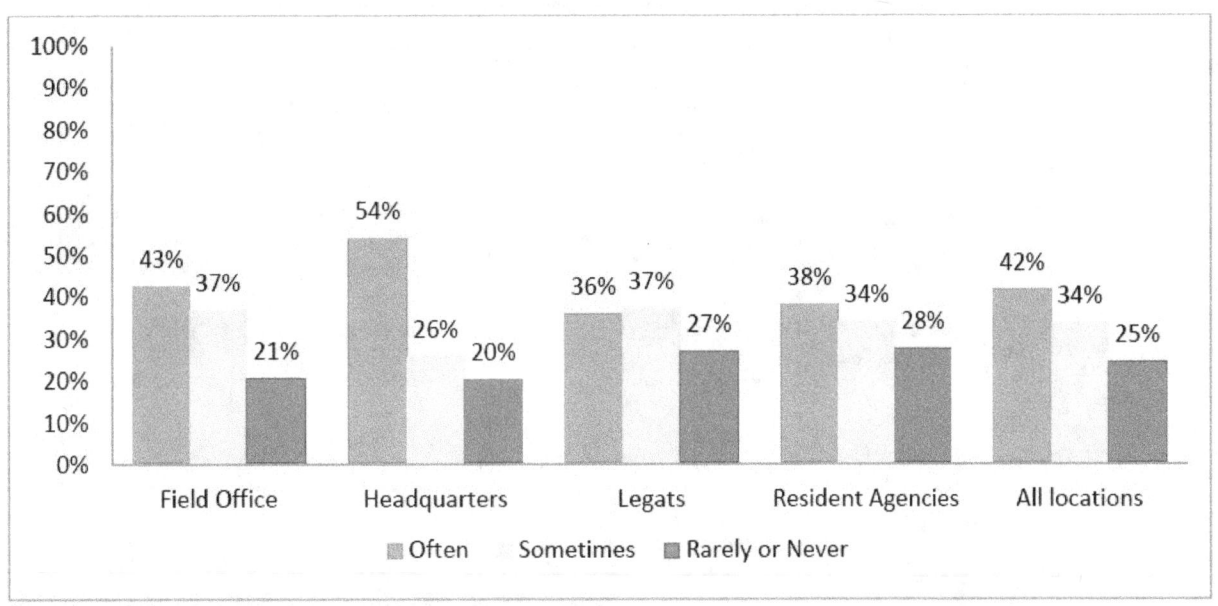

Source: *OIG Analysis of Sentinel User Survey Data*

Similar to many commercial websites, Sentinel includes an advanced search feature that is intended to allow users to narrow the results of searches to meet their specific needs. Overall, we found that 23 percent of participants who used the advanced search functionality reported that they rarely or never received the results they needed. As with the regular search function, a smaller percentage of respondents from FBI field offices, Legats, and Resident Agencies reported they often received the results they needed from advanced search than their colleagues at FBI headquarters.

We also found that respondents did not have high levels of satisfaction with specific aspects of the search function. For example, we found 39 percent of survey respondents reported they were dissatisfied with the organization of information they received when using the search functionality. The level of dissatisfaction varied from 34 percent at FBI headquarters to 46 percent at Legats.

Survey respondents also generally reported difficulty in learning how to use the search function. We found that a higher percentage of users stationed at Legats or Resident Agencies reported difficulty learning to search than their colleagues stationed at FBI headquarters or field offices. Specifically, 48 percent of respondents at Legats and 38 percent of respondents at Resident Agencies reported having difficulty learning how to use Sentinel's search function.[27]

When we compared the number of years survey respondents were employed at the FBI with how easy or difficult they found it to learn how to search in Sentinel, we found that generally the more years of service a respondent had, the more difficult they found it to learn the search function. Exhibit 4 summarizes our analysis.

EXHIBIT 4: EASE IN LEARNING THE SEARCH FEATURE BY FBI TENURE

Tenure	Easy	Neutral	Difficult
More than 20 years	34%	26%	40%
16-20 Years	37%	23%	40%
11-15 Years	39%	18%	43%
6-10 Years	43%	21%	35%
5 Years or Less	55%	21%	24%

Source: OIG Analysis of Sentinel User Survey Data

Finally, we compared the number of hours that respondents reported using Sentinel each week to how easy it was for them to learn to use Sentinel's search function. We found that the number of hours that Sentinel was used per week did not appear to have an impact on whether a user found it easy to learn Sentinel's search function.

---

[27] The following groups were asked how easy or difficult they found it to learn the search function: Special Agents, Operational Support Technicians, and All Other Positions categories.

During our audit, we learned that the FBI had become aware of potential limitations to its search function as early as September 2012, when a report assessing the overall case management function highlighted known limitations of the system's search functionality. That report stated that "the user is now presented with additional search results frequently resulting in information overload. The search engine will sometimes return more results than was desired. Additional tuning or filters are required to balance the false positives and false negatives. ACS had additional algorithms specifically searching for names permutations that Sentinel does not currently support."

Our interviews with Sentinel users and survey results reflected these same concerns. Based on a review of those interviews and results, we found that Sentinel often does not provide users with the search results they need. Sentinel users frequently cited two issues: Sentinel returned too many search results for a person to reasonably review or no results at all for a document the user knew existed. Based on the feedback received from Sentinel users, we are concerned that Sentinel does not appear to have met users' expectations and needs. If users are not provided with a versatile capability to locate different types of information contained within Sentinel, as envisioned in the FBI's stated requirements for Sentinel, there is the potential that an investigation can be hindered because agents or analysts may not be aware of, or may be unable to locate, information that is in Sentinel and relevant to the investigation.

In response to our finding regarding the search function, the Sentinel Program Manager told us that the FBI recognized the need to improve Sentinel's search function and is taking steps to address users' concerns. These efforts include additional training, new algorithms, and other technological improvements to reduce the frequency of false positives and negatives among search results. Additionally, the FBI told us that it intends to improve other search-related features with the deployment of Sentinel 1.5 in October 2014. We have not assessed the impact of these updates on the user experience. In addition to the steps the FBI has already taken to improve the search function, we believe that the FBI should continue to solicit additional and ongoing feedback from Sentinel user groups and use that feedback to enhance the search function.

Indexing

The purpose of the indexing function is to designate, modify, and delete the relationship between any two identifiers, such as the relationship between a person and that person's address. Applying identifiers is intended to allow more precise and comprehensive searching within Sentinel and increase the FBI's ability to "connect the dots." Indexing allows Sentinel users to determine, for example, whether an individual has been the subject of or involved in other investigations. If users do not properly index names and places that arise in FBI investigations, the FBI could provide erroneous and incomplete information to other federal agencies, which could potentially hinder the FBI's and other agencies' ability to efficiently and effectively identify persons of interest who may do harm to the nation.

We found that the primary user concern with Sentinel's indexing function is the amount of administrative burden placed on the author of a document, the person responsible for indexing the document. In our survey, 41 percent of survey respondents reported that they spent more time indexing in Sentinel than they did in ACS.

When the FBI deployed Sentinel, several work processes changed. Under the ACS process, Special Agents marked paper documents with the information they wanted to be indexed and OSTs indexed the documents in ACS. In Sentinel, Special Agents index their own documents rather than assigning it to an administrative staff member. In interviews, Special Agents told us that the increased administrative burden posed by indexing leaves less time for investigative activities. Similarly, as shown in the following exhibit, we found that a greater percentage of respondents outside of FBI headquarters reported that they spent more time on indexing in Sentinel compared to the time they spent indexing in ACS.[28] However, as shown in Exhibit 5, even among the FBI field offices, Legats, and Resident Agencies there was a substantial amount of variation between the percentage of personnel who spent more time on indexing in Sentinel than they did in ACS, with 34 percent of the Legat respondents and 48 percent of the Resident Agency respondents reporting an increase in the amount of time spent on indexing.

EXHIBIT 5: TIME SPENT INDEXING COMPARED TO ACS

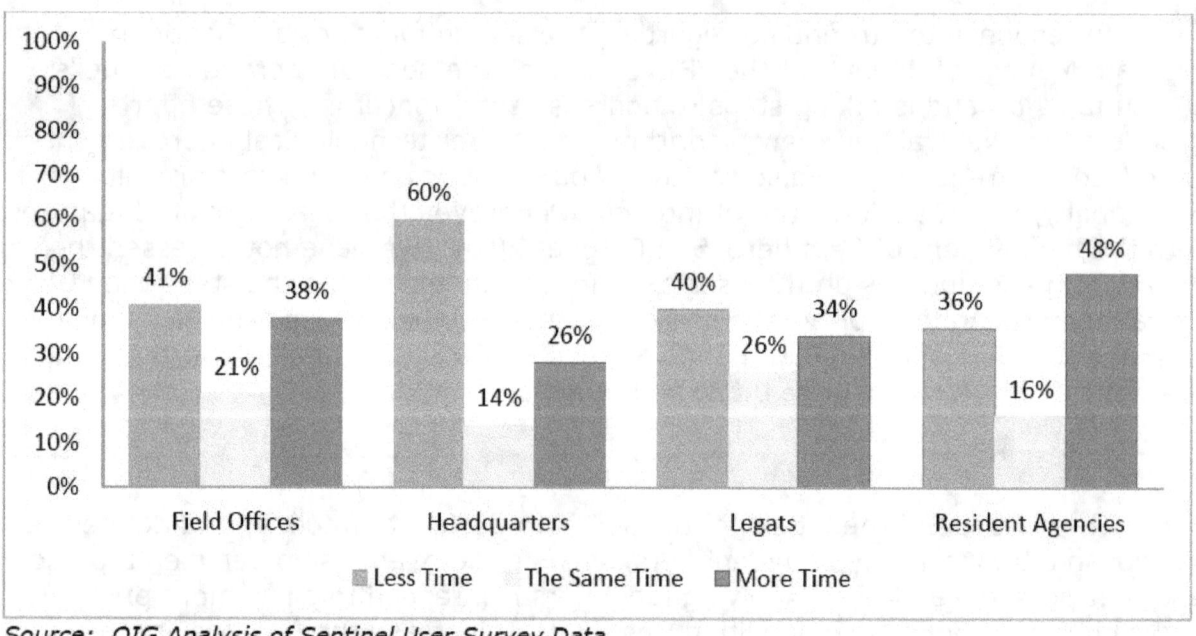

Source: OIG Analysis of Sentinel User Survey Data

---

[28] Forty-six percent of the survey respondents stationed at FBI headquarters responded "Not Applicable," a significantly higher percentage than those stationed at other types of offices, to the question regarding the amount of time spent indexing in Sentinel compared to ACS.

FBI officials told us that the FBI is not currently able to provide Special Agents in the field with assistance in reducing the time it takes to index large structured documents such as bank records, or unstructured documents such as a report of investigation form (FD-302) or email. We believe that the FBI should continue to research technological solutions and review its business processes and policies to identify ways to reduce the time it takes users to index large documents. Because the rate at which documents are being added to Sentinel is substantially greater than the rate the documents were added to ACS and is likely to grow in the future, there is an increasing need for the FBI to address this issue.

Missing Features

To determine whether Sentinel met users' operational needs, we asked survey respondents whether they believed that Sentinel was missing any essential features critical to their duties. Thirty-six percent believed that Sentinel was missing essential features critical to their duties. The two most frequently cited missing features related to Sentinel's integration with other FBI IT systems and survey respondents' desire to see enhancements made to Sentinel's search capability. The responses were similar across most of the job positions with the exception of the ECTs and ELSUR Technicians, 77 percent of whom responded that Sentinel was missing features critical to their duties.[29] While responses from ECTs and ELSUR technicians were only 3 percent of the total responses we received, these technicians use Sentinel to complete a large portion of their duties. Fifty-two percent of ECTs and ELSUR technicians who completed our survey reported using Sentinel more than 30 hours a week.

---

[29] In discussing this issue with FBI management, we were told that users may have been indicating their personal preferences. FBI management stated that it was likely that none of the business processes or information contained within reports was eliminated, but that individuals were likely indicating that they preferred how information was reported in the past.

EXHIBIT 6: RESPONSES TO MISSING FEATURES BY JOB POSITION

Job Position	Yes	No	Don't Know
Supervisory Special Agent	44%	35%	21%
Special Agent	38%	41%	21%
Intelligence Analyst	37%	38%	26%
OST & SST	34%	31%	35%
ECT & ELSUR Technician	77%	19%	3%
All Other Positions	22%	36%	42%
Total	36%	37%	26%

Source: OIG Analysis of Sentinel User Survey Data

We also compared the number of hours survey respondents reported using Sentinel each week to their responses about whether they believed that Sentinel was missing any features essential to their duties. We found that 49 percent of survey respondents who used Sentinel for more than 30 hours per week believed that Sentinel was missing essential features and 33 percent of survey respondents who used Sentinel for 20 hours or less per week thought Sentinel was missing key features. Almost half of the respondents who use Sentinel the most reported that Sentinel is missing features essential to their duties. We believe that the FBI should consider revising how it prioritizes adding new features to Sentinel to account for the needs of those employees who use Sentinel the most.

Finally, we considered whether job-specific training had an effect on respondents' perceptions about whether Sentinel was missing essential features. Since a lack of training could affect a user's knowledge about Sentinel's capabilities and features, we compared survey respondents' views about whether Sentinel was missing features critical to their duties with whether or not they received job-specific Sentinel training. We found that training had a relatively low impact on survey respondents' responses about regarding missing features in Sentinel.

Training and Resources

As part of the transition plan, the FBI offered both training and other types of resources and guides to assist Sentinel users. We found that the majority of survey respondents were generally satisfied with the training and other Sentinel-related resources provided to them.

Prior to Sentinel's deployment in July 2012, the FBI identified and provided job-specific training to employees most affected by the transition to Sentinel.[30] Overall, the majority of survey respondents reported they had received Sentinel training that was specific to their job responsibilities prior to the deployment of Sentinel. However, only 38 percent of the Intelligence Analysts, the lowest percentage of any of the positions we surveyed, reported having received job-specific training. Of those who received the training, 58 percent were satisfied or very satisfied with the usefulness of the training and 26 percent were neutral. Some survey respondents stated in their narrative responses to our survey that more Sentinel training is needed.

In addition to job-specific training, the FBI developed and established several types of training resources and guides to assist Sentinel users, including local Sentinel coordinators, Sentinel Quick Guides, and Sentinel frequently asked questions (FAQ) lists.[31] The majority of survey respondents were aware that these resources and guides were available to them. More than 50 percent of respondents who reported using these resources found them to be very helpful or helpful. In addition, at least 22 percent of respondents found these resources to be somewhat helpful. The highest rated of these resources was the Sentinel coordinator, with 69 percent of survey respondents reporting that they were very helpful or helpful.

We asked survey respondents to indicate how satisfied or dissatisfied they were with the availability of technical support, policy-related support, and basic user support. Technical support relates to defects or bugs in the system, policy-related support provides guidance on the use of Sentinel in accordance with FBI policy, and basic user support provides guidance on how to perform basic tasks in Sentinel. Our survey results indicated that overall, 53 percent of survey respondents reported that they are satisfied with the availability of basic user support assistance. However, only 33 percent of Special Agents and 27 percent of Supervisory Special Agents who responded to the survey reported being satisfied with the availability of policy-related support. In addition, only 38 percent of Special Agents and 30 percent of Supervisory Special Agents were satisfied with the availability of Sentinel system defect-related technical support.

---

[30] The Sentinel training program was designed for FBI personnel who use or support Sentinel. According to the FBI, training goals were designed to provide an overall understanding of the scope and purpose of Sentinel, create a positive image of the Sentinel program and its benefits, and provide users with opportunities to gain hands-on experience with the functions in Sentinel that they will use to perform their jobs.

[31] Sentinel coordinators are FBI employees located in field offices who were trained by the Sentinel team. They are the local resources for Sentinel users who require assistance using the system. Quick guides are short instructional guides that are posted on the FBI Intranet. Sample topics include: getting started, online help, how to create a document, how to use new and revised forms, and the workflow process. The Sentinel FAQ list includes functionality enhancements and techniques for improving the user experience or improving efficiency in working with Sentinel.

Impact of Change on Business Processes

In 2009, the FBI initiated a Field Administrative Workload Study on Special Agents to identify: (1) the amount of time dedicated to administrative tasks, (2) the amount of time spent on problematic (i.e., inefficient or ineffective) tasks, and (3) the types of tasks that require the majority of their time to determine the prevailing tasks and issues that hinder Special Agents' ability to focus on non-administrative investigative and intelligence case work.[32] The FBI found that Special Agents were spending 36 percent of their time on administrative tasks, which were defined as tasks that non-Special Agent employees could accomplish. Partly in response to the findings of that study, the FBI created the operational support technician (OST) position to provide administrative and technical support to both investigative and administrative squads in an FBI field office.

Based upon our fieldwork and survey results, we determined that prior to the deployment of Sentinel, many OSTs spent a significant amount of their time on tasks related to the indexing process. Since the deployment of Sentinel, Special Agents have indexed their own cases. This reduction in the scope of work typically performed by OSTs creates an opportunity for the OSTs to perform additional administrative tasks, which both ensures that OSTs are fully utilized and reduces the administrative burden on Special Agents in the field. However, during our interviews, the OSTs stated that they were not always used efficiently or assigned new tasks to replace the time they previously spent indexing. Special Agents' and OSTs' responses to some of the open-ended survey questions similarly expressed the concern that OSTs are underutilized because their work was transferred to Special Agents. We also noted during our analysis of the open-ended survey questions that for those who stated that their daily productivity decreased, 55 percent of Special Agents attributed the decrease to administrative burden. Based upon these findings, we are concerned that OSTs may not be utilized fully and consistently throughout all FBI field offices.

In response to our concerns about OSTs, the FBI provided us with documentation of the training that was previously given to Administrative Officers and Assistant Special Agents-in-Charge that describes the tasks that OSTs can perform in Sentinel, which include re-indexing information, processing leads and evidence returns, assisting Special Agents with managing cases, and assisting with other administrative tasks. The January 2013 training documentation also stated that it is possible that not every squad will need an OST and that offices should assess their workloads and reallocate positions accordingly. According to the FBI, many offices have conducted such assessments to determine the workload and training needs of OSTs. We have not assessed the impact of this training on the utilization of OSTs and therefore we cannot comment on the outcome of the FBI's efforts. In addition to the steps the FBI has already taken to improve the utilization of OSTs, we recommend that the FBI evaluate the progress that FBI field offices

---

[32] The study included GS-10 through GS-13 Special Agents assigned to field offices and Resident Agencies.

have made in ensuring that OSTs are fully and effectively performing administrative tasks within Sentinel to optimally reduce the administrative responsibilities of Special Agents.

Security

The Sentinel system requirements stipulate that Sentinel will provide the capability to control access based upon user roles, in addition to allowing FBI leadership at FBI headquarters and in the field to define user roles and responsibilities to fit their records management operating procedures. To determine whether Sentinel users believed that the system access controls were sufficient, we asked them to confirm whether they believed that they were able to exceed their authority in Sentinel. We analyzed user survey responses and found that 83 percent of survey respondents did not believe that Sentinel allowed them to exceed their authority. Another 13 percent responded that they did not know whether Sentinel allowed them to exceed their authority and 4 percent believed Sentinel did.[33]

In 2013, the OIG contracted with KPMG LLP to perform a separate audit of Sentinel in accordance with the Federal Information Security Management Act of FY 2002.[34] KPMG LLP evaluated controls from 6 of the 18 control areas identified in the National Institute of Standards and Technology Special Publication 800-53 Revision 3, August 2009, *Recommended Security Controls for Federal Information Security Systems and Organizations.*[35]

KPMG LLP's June 014 report identified deficiencies in 2 of the 6 control areas tested. These 2 control areas pertained to Risk Assessment and to Audit and Accountability. KPMG LLP concluded that these deficiencies exist because the FBI did not consistently develop and enforce information technology security policies for the system in accordance with current FBI and National Institute of Standards and Technology policies and procedures. KPMG LLP provided two recommendations for

---

[33] In response to these findings, FBI officials told us that it is aware of one instance where access control was a concern and in that instance the cause was a user error issue and not a Sentinel issue. FBI officials further told us that there are some users who believe that only the case agent should have access to the information contained in a case file even though Sentinel was designed to facilitate information sharing. They believe this view could have led some survey respondents to believe that Sentinel has allowed them to exceed their authority.

[34] U.S. Department of Justice Office of the Inspector General, *Audit of the Federal Bureau of Investigation's Sentinel Pursuant to the Federal Information Security Management Act, Fiscal Year 2013*, Audit Report 14-25 (June 2014). This report is classified; however, the text herein is unclassified.

[35] The selected controls included common security controls and other controls critical to a system that is likely to change over time, such as technical controls that are subject to the direct effects of frequent changes in hardware software components. KPMG LLP selected specific test procedures that were applicable to the computing environment; therefore, not all control areas were evaluated.

improving the security posture of the Sentinel control environment and FBI management concurred with the recommendations.

Sentinel Budget

As of July 2014, the FBI reported it had obligated $432 million of the $451 million available for Sentinel at the time Sentinel 1.0 was deployed. The total budget for Sentinel since the deployment of Sentinel 1.0 in July 2012 has increased from $451 million to $551.4 million. This increase is the result of operations and maintenance during FY 2013 and 2014 and the development of new functionality during FY 2014. As of July 2014, the FBI had obligated $529.2 million of that $551.4 million and expensed $502.1 million.[36]

EXHIBIT 7: SENTINEL DEVELOPMENT AND O&M BUDGET

Sentinel Development and O&M Budget (March 2006 – September 2014)						
Sentinel Release	Development Budget	O&M Budget	Total Budget Development and O&M	Amount Obligated (As of JUL 23, 2014)	Amount Expensed (As of JUL 23, 2014)	Remaining Funds thru SEP 14, 2014
Sentinel 1.0 (MAR 2006 – JUL 2012)	$451M	-	$451M	($431.7M)	($431.7M)	-
Sentinel 1.1 to 1.4 (JUL 2012 – SEP 2013)	-	$58.5M	$58.5M	($60M)[37]	($54.3M)	-
Sentinel 1.5 (OCT 2013 – SEP 2014)	$12.3M	$29.6M	$41.9M	($37.5M)	($16.1)	-
Total Budget	$463.3M	$88.1M	$551.4M	($529.2M)	($502.1)	$4.5M

Source: FBI Finance Division

Sentinel Enhancements

The FBI has updated the Sentinel application several times since it was deployed in July 2012. These updates include "bug" fixes, user interface updates,

---

[36] As of March 2014, the FBI reported it had obligated $432 million of the $451 million available for Sentinel in FY 2012 at the time Sentinel 1.0 was deployed. However, as discussed in our December 2011 and September 2012 reports, these obligated and budgeted amounts did not include costs for 2 years of operations and maintenance after Sentinel was completed, costs that were part of the $451 million cost estimate that the FBI projected for Sentinel in 2008.

[37] The FBI used carryover authority to transfer FY 2011 available balances to No Year funding for 2012 Sentinel requirements. As a result, during FY 2012 the FBI had the ability to obligate more than the amount appropriated to Sentinel.

performance improvements, user experience improvements, and additional changes in response to user feedback.[38]

Sentinel 1.1, 1.2, and 1.3 releases were deployed to users in September 2012, December 2012 and February 2013, respectively, and included:

- improved indexing, resolving an issue where documents from external systems (i.e., Delta) would have to be re-indexed in Sentinel and adding indexing templates (name, aliases date of birth, citizenship, languages) to improve the sufficiency of indexing;

- improved response time when retrieving documents from large cases;

- created default access control restrictions for some case classifications;

- refined the capability to search for images;

- refined the workflow for entering evidence into Sentinel;

- added the capability to create the physical surveillance request (FD-1054) and physical surveillance log (FD-1055) forms within Sentinel using Sentinel's workflow;

- added the capability to limit a search to a specific case and subfiles contained in the case; and

- improved search accuracy, including a revised set of stop words.[39]

Sentinel 1.4 was deployed in September 2013. It included fixes related to evidence functionality, forms, search functionality, indexing and entity management, and serialization and accomplishment functionality.

The FBI provided the OIG with documentation outlining its development plans for Sentinel 1.5, which is being developed to support the needs of the FBI's Intelligence Analysts and is scheduled to be deployed in October 2014. Because Sentinel 1.5 is directed toward the needs of Intelligence Analysts, the Sentinel development team is working together with subject matter experts from the Directorate of Intelligence (DI) to design and deploy a functionality that will meet the needs of the analysts. Sentinel 1.5 will consolidate the Collection Operation

---

[38] FBI Enterprise Requirements and Capabilities Working Group reviews and prioritizes requests, obtains the technical level of effort from the Sentinel team, validates the release schedule, and submits the release schedule to the Executive Steering Council for review. This process is intended to focus the Sentinel team's efforts on business priorities and scheduling work that is within resource capacity.

[39] Stop words are words ignored by a search engine when matching queries to results. They comprise the most commonly occurring words in a language, such as a, an, or and.

and Requirements Environment (CORE) and the FBI Intelligence Information Report Dissemination System (FIDS) into Sentinel, enhance Sentinel interface with Delta, and enable a Sentinel-iData interface. The FBI is employing an Agile development methodology for designing and implementing this enhanced functionality. The FBI has said it will identify enhancements to existing system functionality, including work item authoring, search, and workflow to continue to support the FBI's intelligence mission. According to the FBI, the consolidation of these legacy systems will simplify the user experience, retire legacy investments resulting in cost avoidance, reduce time to awareness, and increase data availability.

The FBI plans to deploy Sentinel 1.5's new capabilities using the same model that was used to transition from ACS to Sentinel 1.0. The plan includes training FBI personnel at FBI headquarters and in the field, developing user guides and a FAQ list, and developing an FBI headquarters based team responsible for assessing and responding to user questions or concerns. However, the transition effort will be scaled down in comparison to the transition from ACS because Sentinel 1.5 will primarily affect Intelligence Analysts.

Conclusion

Two years have passed since the FBI deployed Sentinel to users in July 2012. Since the deployment, the FBI has worked to improve both the functionality and user's experience with Sentinel. During our audit, we found that the majority of users who participated in our survey viewed their experience with Sentinel positively, responding that Sentinel has increased their daily productivity, increased their ability to share information with personnel in other offices, and enhanced the FBI's ability to carry out its mission. Some survey respondents also stated that Sentinel is an improvement over ACS. However, ECTs and ELSUR Technicians expressed concerns about the impact Sentinel had on their daily work activities that play a vital role in the storage and management of evidence collected by the FBI. In addition, we found that survey respondents' satisfaction with Sentinel's search and indexing functionality was significantly lower than other functions because they did not reliably receive the search results they needed and reported spending too much of their time manually indexing information. FBI officials are aware of these concerns and told us that they plan to address them.

The deployment of Sentinel represented significant changes in both the technology and business processes used by FBI employees to accomplish tasks. Of those Special Agents who responded that Sentinel had decreased their daily productivity, a majority attributed the productivity decrease to an increase in administrative burden. During our audit, Special Agents told us that the increase in the administrative burden posed by indexing leaves less time for investigative activities. Prior to the deployment of Sentinel, OSTs played a significant role in the indexing process. Since the deployment of Sentinel, that role has been eliminated, creating an opportunity for OSTs to potentially ease the increased administrative burden on Special Agents in the field. However, we found that OSTs were not always used efficiently or assigned new tasks to supplant their previous indexing duties. As a result, we believe that some user concerns, especially those relating to indexing, may require both a technical and business process solution.

Survey respondents' also reported that Sentinel was missing features that they believed are critical to their duties, such as Sentinel's integration with other FBI IT systems and enhancements to the search capability. Enhanced search capabilities should improve user satisfaction with Sentinel and increase the FBI's ability to "connect the dots." To ensure that future enhancements are more aligned with user's operational needs, the FBI should consider revising how it prioritizes the addition of new enhancements to the system. In addition, although respondents were generally satisfied with the job-specific training and other resources the FBI offered, Special Agents and Supervisory Special Agents reported a significantly lower level of satisfaction with the availability of technical and policy-related support after the deployment of Sentinel.

The total budget for Sentinel since the deployment of Sentinel 1.0 in July 2012 has increased from $451 million to $551.4 million. This increase is the result of operations and maintenance during FY 2013 and 2014 and the development of new functionality during FY 2014. As of July 2014, the FBI had obligated $529.2 million of that $551.4 million and expensed $502.1 million. The FBI's deployment of Sentinel 1.5, planned for October 2014, is intended to support the needs of the FBI's intelligence analysts by integrating legacy intelligence systems and expanding Sentinel's functionality by leveraging its features to support the FBI's intelligence mission. If Sentinel 1.5 successfully subsumes other legacy systems or improves the integration of Sentinel with other legacy systems, the FBI should realize cost savings from retiring systems and reducing the amount of maintenance to operate other legacy systems.

Recommendations

We recommend that the FBI:

1. Evaluate the progress that FBI field offices have made in ensuring that OSTs are fully and effectively performing administrative tasks within Sentinel to optimally reduce the administrative responsibilities of Special Agents.

2. Solicit user feedback on Sentinel to ensure improvements made to the search function adequately reflect user needs.

3. Continue to research technological solutions and review business processes and policies to identify ways to reduce the time it takes users to index large unstructured documents.

STATEMENT ON INTERNAL CONTROLS

As required by the *Government Auditing Standards*, we tested, as appropriate, internal controls significant within the context of our audit objectives. A deficiency in an internal control exists when the design or operation of a control does not allow management or employees, in the normal course of performing their assigned functions, to timely prevent or detect: (1) impairments to the effectiveness and efficiency of operations, (2) misstatements in financial or performance information, or (3) violations of laws and regulations. Our evaluation of the Federal Bureau of Investigation's internal controls was *not* made for the purpose of providing assurance on its internal control structure as a whole. FBI management is responsible for the establishment and maintenance of internal controls.

Through our audit testing, we did not identify any deficiencies in the FBI's internal controls that are significant within the context of the audit objectives and based upon the audit work performed that we believe would affect the FBI's ability to effectively and efficiently operate, to correctly state financial and performance information, and to ensure compliance with laws and regulations.

Because we are not expressing an opinion on the FBI's internal control structure as a whole, this statement is intended solely for the information and use of the FBI. This restriction is not intended to limit the distribution of this report, which is a matter of public record.

STATEMENT ON COMPLIANCE
WITH LAWS AND REGULATIONS

As required by the *Government Auditing Standards* we tested, as appropriate given our audit scope and objectives, selected transactions, records, procedures, and practices, to obtain reasonable assurance that the Federal Bureau of Investigation's (FBI) management complied with federal laws and regulations, for which noncompliance, in our judgment, could have a material effect on the results of our audit. FBI's management is responsible for ensuring compliance with applicable federal laws and regulations. In planning our audit, we identified the following laws and regulations that concerned the operations of the auditee and that were significant within the context of the audit objectives:

- FBI Domestic Investigations and Operations Guide dated October 15, 2011; and
- Executive Order 13388: Further Strengthening the Sharing of Terrorism Information to Protect Americans, dated October 25, 2005.

Our audit included examining, on a test basis, the FBI's compliance with the aforementioned laws and regulations that could have a material effect on the FBI's operations, through interviewing FBI personnel, analyzing survey data and reviewing program contract and budget documentation. Nothing came to our attention that caused us to believe that the FBI was not in compliance with the aforementioned laws and regulations.

OBJECTIVE, SCOPE, AND METHODOLOGY

Objectives

The objectives of this audit were to examine Sentinel's effect on FBI daily operations and its ability to expand users' search capabilities, thereby enhancing agents' and analysts' ability to link cases with similar information and share that information with other law enforcement agencies with a need to know in order to solve cases efficiently. We also reviewed Sentinel's current project costs in addition to Sentinel's completed and planned functionality since it was deployed.

Scope and Methodology

We conducted this performance audit in accordance with generally accepted government auditing standards. Those standards require that we plan and perform the audit to obtain sufficient, appropriate evidence to provide a reasonable basis for our findings and conclusions based on our audit objectives. We believe that the evidence obtained provides a reasonable based for our findings and conclusions based on our audit objectives

Our audit focused on users' experiences with Sentinel's functionality and their ability to effectively and efficiently enter, search, and share information in the FBI's case management system. The scope of our review primarily encompasses January 2013 through December 2013.

To accomplish our audit objective, we interviewed Sentinel users, we used a survey to assess user satisfaction with the system, examined Sentinel costs incurred and budgeted, and reviewed improvements made to Sentinel as well as improvements planned for Sentinel. We interviewed Sentinel users at FBI headquarters in Washington, DC, and the FBI field offices in Baltimore, MD; Charlotte, NC; Newark, NJ; and Philadelphia, PA.

We designed the Sentinel user survey based on the results of these interviews. At the time of the survey design, the FBI employees' database contained 36,114 employees with FBINet e-mail accounts that can only be accessed within FBI's network. The software used to deploy the survey resides on a Department of Justice (DOJ) server and the link to the survey could not be sent through the FBINet e-mail accounts from the DOJ server. The sample universe was then reduced to the 13,989 employees with UNet e-mail accounts who can access the survey from the DOJ server.

To provide appropriate coverage of these e-mail account holders at FBI headquarters, field offices, Resident Agencies, and Legal Attaché offices, we employed a stratified sample design. In some Resident Agencies, there were four or less employees with UNet email accounts. For these Resident Agencies, all of their 426 employees with UNet email accounts were included in the survey sample. The same approach was used for the 210 ECT, ELSUR Technician, OST/SST positions and the 202 Legat employees, all of which had low numbers of employees with UNet email accounts. A representative random sample of 1,675 users was selected from the remaining universe covering FBI headquarters, field offices, and Resident Agencies.

The following tables show the distribution of the above selected 2,513 survey recipients and respondents by (a) the types of FBI office they work and (b) the employees' position titles within their respective offices:

| FBI Office Type | Employees | Number of Survey | | Response Rate |
		Recipients	Respondents	
Headquarters	4,030	551	209	38%
Field Offices	7,232	821	358	44%
Resident Agencies	2,525	939	494	53%
Legats	202	202	89	44%
Total	**13,989**	**2,513**	**1,150**	**46%**

| Position Title | Number of Survey | | Response Rate |
	Recipients	Respondents	
Special Agents	1,027	503	49%
All Other Position Titles	671	257	38%
Supervisory Special Agents	423	185	44%
Intelligence Analysts	182	91	50%
Operational Support & Support Services Technicians	158	83	53%
ECTs & ELSUR Technicians	52	31	60%
Total	**2,513**	**1,150**	**46%**

The Sentinel survey recipients were placed into four main groups based on the FBI employees' position titles in order to capture relevant information about the various functionalities of Sentinel. There were four different questionnaires deployed to each of the following position title groups: (1) Special Agents, (2) Supervisory Special Agents, (3) Technicians, and (4) All Other Position Titles. The questionnaires generally contained the same questions, except some job-specific questions that varied based on their job duties. The survey was deployed between November 5, 2013, and December 4, 2013.

We reviewed the responses and performed descriptive and statistical analyses using the Statistical Product and Service Solutions software package.

The practical difficulties of conducting any survey introduce various types of errors related to survey responses. For example, differences in how a particular question is interpreted and differences in the sources of information available to respondents can be sources of error. In addition, respondents might not be uniformly conscientious in expressing their views or they may be influenced by concerns about how their answers might be viewed by the OIG, the FBI, or the public. We included steps intended to minimize such errors. For example, to address differences in how questions were interpreted, we pre-tested our survey with 41 FBI employees at FBI headquarters and 4 field offices. We modified our survey questions based on the results of these pre-tests. In addition, we incorporated comments from the FBI about the content and clarity of our survey.

When we analyzed the results of our survey, we verified the results we obtained by using our survey software by exporting the data to another software program and performing the same analysis. The summary of our survey responses are contained in Appendix II.

We interviewed the FBI Chief Financial Officer and Sentinel Contracting Officers. We also reviewed staffing charts, contract modifications, bridge contracts and related invoices, award documentation, operations and maintenance expenditures, and overall historical spending documentation to determine the costs incurred as well as the status of the Sentinel budget.

RESULTS OF ALL SENTINEL SURVEYS EXCLUDING RESPONDENTS' BACKGROUND QUESTIONS

How easy or difficult was it for you to learn how to perform the following tasks in Sentinel?	Very Easy	Easy	Neither Easy Nor Difficult	Difficult	Very Difficult	Not Applicable	Total
Indexing	121	336	255	227	80	122	1141
Search	111	268	190	195	113	48	925
Advanced search	90	214	182	177	111	71	845
Set a lead to another office	162	397	164	68	13	125	929
Set a lead within your office	167	389	164	55	10	145	930
Drafting a Form	176	349	146	48	8	117	844
Approving a Form	106	166	69	20	3	166	530
Importing Forms	50	100	53	24	4	115	346
Adding an Attachment	57	122	67	16	5	80	347
Drafting a Complaint Form (FD-71)	84	217	170	55	9	390	925
Drafting an EC (FD-1057)	232	394	128	47	10	40	851
Drafting an FD-302	182	229	67	10	0	13	501
Request to Open a Case	126	220	88	41	5	22	502
Request to Close a Case	109	184	113	43	9	40	498
Approving a Lead to Another Office	58	80	31	5	1	9	184
Approving a Lead Within Your Office	61	79	28	6	2	9	185
Approving an EC (FD-1057)	127	167	63	18	5	150	530
Approving an FD-302	68	59	22	4	1	30	184
Approving the Opening of a Case	62	67	32	7	1	15	184
Approving the Closing of a Case	55	72	29	7	1	21	185
Destruction of evidence for closed cases	1	0	3	0	0	0	4
Updating chain of custody	1	2	0	1	0	0	4
Evidence log (FD-192)	6	15	5	4	0	0	30
FD-940s (Title III request form)	0	0	1	0	1	2	4
Barcode system	7	8	8	3	1	0	27
Chain of custody related functions	5	6	4	9	3	0	27
Separating evidence (split function)	3	3	6	7	7	0	26
Inventory tasks	1	0	3	6	10	6	26
Stat reviews	6	21	13	8	4	30	82
Data queries	6	29	18	12	7	8	80
Case migration	14	32	12	3	1	19	81
Serialization transfers	13	22	13	7	1	25	81
Lead requests	11	36	16	2	1	16	82

Compared to the process with ACS, how much more or less time do you spend completing the following tasks in Sentinel?	Significantly Less Time	Less Time	The Same Time	More Time	Significantly More Time	Not Applicable	Total
Indexing	122	249	163	222	154	191	1101
Searching	49	111	80	70	43	71	424
Drafting a Complaint form (FD-71)	71	190	162	87	14	391	915
Drafting a form	100	274	224	67	19	154	838
Drafting an EC (FD-1057)	144	309	219	76	20	79	847
Drafting an FD-302	83	174	144	69	14	17	501
Evidence log (FD-192)	3	7	3	8	7	2	30
FD-940s (Title III request form)	0	0	1	0	1	2	4
Importing Forms	40	94	43	13	6	147	343
Separating evidence (split function)	3	1	7	8	5	2	26
Serialization transfers	7	13	18	16	5	22	81
Set a lead to another office	157	314	195	80	22	159	927
Set a lead within your office	154	301	202	72	16	183	928
Stat reviews	7	20	8	7	7	33	82
Updating chain of custody	0	1	1	0	2	0	4
Inventory tasks	1	0	1	2	14	9	27
Lead requests	10	22	27	2	1	20	82
Request to close a case	85	170	120	62	14	46	497
Request to open a case	84	188	122	61	16	29	500
Approving a lead to another office	40	61	46	21	3	12	183
Approving a lead within your office	40	60	53	16	1	14	184
Approving an EC (FD-1057)	79	141	87	34	9	177	527
Approving an FD-302	39	50	41	16	2	33	181
Approving the Closing of a Case	39	52	50	17	3	22	183
Approving the Opening of a Case	39	60	40	23	4	17	183
Adding attachments	53	100	49	13	9	121	345
Approving a Form	65	128	92	34	8	199	526
Barcode system	3	0	10	11	0	2	26
Case migration	6	16	13	6	3	37	81
Chain of custody related functions	3	3	1	7	11	2	27
Cover a lead	114	208	128	33	4	15	502
Data queries	7	20	19	14	8	12	80
Destruction of evidence for closed cases	0	3	0	0	1	0	4
Disposing of evidence for closed cases	4	5	8	8	3	3	31
To get documents approved	266	273	123	97	29	63	851

How responsive or slow is Sentinel when you are performing the following functions?	Very Slow	Slow	Neither Responsive Nor Slow	Responsive	Very Responsive	Not Applicable	Total
Indexing	37	139	249	410	150	139	1124
Search	16	64	77	164	50	53	424
Advanced search	13	47	58	113	38	73	342
Set a lead to another office	9	62	185	343	132	117	848
Set a lead within your office	7	61	187	315	142	130	842
Drafting a Form	8	69	168	315	144	136	840
Approving a Form	4	23	85	151	80	182	525
Importing Forms	5	20	52	106	39	121	343
Adding an Attachment(s)	3	19	64	120	43	98	347
Drafting a Complaint Form (FD-71)	7	55	150	234	100	352	898
Drafting an EC (FD-1057)	11	82	164	371	165	49	842
Drafting an FD-302	5	43	98	228	117	10	501
Request to Open a Case	5	38	105	228	101	22	499
Request to Close a Case	4	43	108	214	96	34	499
Approving a Lead to Another Office	2	11	41	87	31	13	185
Approving a Lead Within Your Office	2	9	42	86	33	12	184
Approving an EC (FD-1057)	7	24	87	181	75	151	525
Approving an FD-302	4	6	35	72	34	32	183
Approving the Opening of a Case	2	10	39	85	31	18	185
Approving the Closing of a Case	3	10	37	80	32	22	184
Destruction of evidence for closed cases	0	0	2	2	0	0	4
Updating chain of custody	1	1	1	1	0	0	4
Evidence log (FD-192)	3	6	8	13	1	0	31
FD-940s (Title III request form)	0	1	1	0	0	2	4
Barcode system	3	3	6	13	2	0	27
Chain of custody related functions	6	6	2	12	1	0	27
Separating evidence (split function)	2	4	3	16	1	0	26
Inventory tasks	7	4	5	4	0	7	27
Stat reviews	3	6	12	24	3	34	82
Data queries	1	11	16	34	7	12	81
Case migration	3	12	17	21	4	24	81
Serialization transfers	2	7	15	26	6	25	81
Lead requests	1	3	20	32	8	18	82

How satisfied or dissatisfied are you with the:	Very Satisfied	Satisfied	Neither satisfied Nor Dissatisfied	Dissatisfied	Very Dissatisfied	Not Applicable	Total
transition from ACS to Sentinel	166	564	249	140	31	NA	1150
privileges assigned to your user role in Sentinel	165	630	261	61	12	21	1150
organization of information generated from Search	81	350	229	271	153	66	1150
organization of information generated from Advance Search	74	343	226	248	125	134	1150
organization of information generated from Reports	68	273	238	114	75	382	1150
appearance of the "Resolution" features displayed on the Sentinel user interface	165	619	234	52	28	23	1121
appearance of the "Font Size" features displayed on the Sentinel user interface	155	568	217	104	49	23	1116
usefulness of the training you received that was specific to your job	79	353	195	87	31	12	757
availability of policy-related technical support for Sentinel	48	206	318	95	37	442	1146
availability of basic user assistance (how-to) related technical support for Sentinel	86	391	306	89	33	241	1146
availability of user-error related technical support for Sentinel	64	299	330	92	38	323	1146
availability of system defects or bugs related technical support for Sentinel	57	252	325	113	53	346	1146
assistance that was provided to you for policy-related support	25	150	140	46	17	766	1144
assistance that was provided to you for basic user assistance (how-to)	79	355	171	44	20	476	1145
assistance that was provided to you for user-error related support	54	236	179	45	22	608	1144
assistance that was provided to you for system defects or bugs related support	36	198	173	68	42	627	1144
structure of the collaboration function within Sentinel	63	272	113	105	8	NA	561

Compared to ACS, how have the following characteristics in your unit's most common work product(s) improved or declined since you started using Sentinel?	Significant Improvement	Some Improvement	No Change	Some Decline	Significant Decline	Don't Know	Total
Completeness	283	354	318	53	29	113	1150
Accuracy	239	329	342	85	34	121	1150
Misplaced documentation	284	258	263	89	55	201	1150

Overall, how often were the following forms of technical support for Sentinel able to resolve your issues?	Very Often	Often	Sometimes	Rarely	Never	Not Applicable	Total
Policy-related support	35	108	101	74	49	779	1146
Basic user assistance (how-to)	97	257	201	79	27	485	1146
User-error related support	69	175	164	91	32	615	1146
System defects or bugs	44	136	163	102	53	648	1146

How often do the following Sentinel functions provide you with the results you need?	Very Often	Often	Sometimes	Rarely	Never	Not Applicable	Total
Search	99	352	365	231	34	69	1150
Advanced Search	93	321	366	201	36	133	1150
Reports	86	253	251	129	43	388	1150

As a resource for using Sentinel, how helpful or unhelpful are each of the following?	Very Helpful	Helpful	Somewhat Helpful	Unhelpful	Not at All Helpful	Not Used	Total
Local Sentinel coordinator	225	302	168	42	27	382	1146
Sentinel Quick Guides	93	332	246	42	16	417	1146
Sentinel Interactive Demonstration	56	195	168	45	18	663	1145
Sentinel Training Videos	57	186	174	48	24	656	1145
Sentinel FAQs List	88	285	277	43	19	434	1146

Do you use any of the following IT systems:	Yes	No	Total
Delta	644	506	1150
FIDS	106	1044	1150
CORE	585	565	1150
Compass	144	1006	1150
IDW	453	697	1150
None of the above	307	842	1149

Are you aware of the following resources or guides on Sentinel?	Yes	No	Total
Local Sentinel coordinator	826	320	1146
Sentinel Quick Guides	866	280	1146
Sentinel Interactive Demonstration	637	509	1146
Sentinel Training Videos	704	441	1145
Sentinel FAQs List	852	293	1145

When using Sentinel, do you know who to contact to receive assistance for the following forms of technical support?	Yes	No	Total
Policy-related support	436	708	1144
Basic user assistance (how-to)	770	376	1146
User-error related support	619	527	1146
System defects or bugs	575	570	1145

Question	Yes	No	Don't Know	Not Applicable	Total
Was your unit provided with all the necessary equipment to use Sentinel effectively when it was deployed in July 2012?	852	256	NA	42	1150
In the last 90 days, do you believe that Sentinel has allowed you to exceed your authority to see information that you were not intended to?	43	952	153	NA	1148
Is Sentinel missing any essential features that you believe are critical to your duties?	417	429	303	NA	1149
Are there circumstances where you perform a mandatory paper process in addition to a digital process within Sentinel?	503	489	NA	154	1146
Does the paper product have any evidentiary or substantial value that the digital product may not?	252	188	67	NA	507
Did you receive any Sentinel training that was specific to your job responsibilities when Sentinel was deployed in July 2012?	747	399	NA	NA	1146
Have you served in an acting capacity since Sentinel was deployed in July 2012?	379	657	NA	NA	1036
Did you continue to have access privileges intended for the person you were acting for after you were no longer acting in that role?	112	246	NA	23	381
Have you ever used the collaboration function within Sentinel?	552	124	NA	12	688
Have you received a lead in Sentinel in which you were not the intended recipient?	381	618	NA	37	1036
Are you able to record in Sentinel the date and time of when the evidence was actually repackaged?	5	10	7	NA	22
Are you aware of any Standard Operating Procedures (SOPs) for updating the digital (i.e. Sentinel) and the paper chains of custody?	9	18	NA	NA	27
Have you encountered data integrity issues such as data disappearing or not appearing as it should on the screen when sending forms through Sentinel?	35	59	NA	20	114
Have you performed the task of repackaging evidence?	22	4	NA	1	27

Question	Very Often	Often	Sometimes	Rarely	Never	Not Applicable	Total
How often have you received a lead not intended for you?	31	45	132	169	7	16	400
How often do you receive notifications in Sentinel that do not apply to you?	151	169	186	123	47	10	686
How often do you receive ELSUR technician-related notifications in Sentinel?	21	3	0	0	0	3	27
How often do you receive evidence technician-related notifications in Sentinel?	3	0	0	1	0	0	4
Compared to ACS, how often have there been discrepancies when using Sentinel for ELSUR evidence charged out?	0	1	0	0	2	1	4

Question	Very Easy	Easy	Neither Easy Nor Difficult	Difficult	Very Difficult	Not Applicable	Total
How easy or difficult is it to navigate the Sentinel user interface (display on the monitor)?	220	588	236	64	18	23	1149
Compared to the process with ACS, how easy or difficult is it to locate pieces of evidence search for evidence using Sentinel?	0	4	3	13	5	2	27

Question	Increased a Lot	Increased Some	No Difference	Decreased Some	Decreased a Lot	Not Applicable	Total
Compared to ACS, to what extent has Sentinel increased or decreased your daily productivity?	233	399	232	140	86	60	1150
How has your ability to share information with colleagues who are not located in your office changed since you started using Sentinel?	322	334	257	26	11	86	1036

Question	Strongly Agree	Agree	Neither Agree Nor Disagree	Disagree	Strongly Disagree	Total
Do you agree or disagree that users need Sentinel training prior to using Sentinel?	465	528	114	36	3	1146
How strongly do you agree or disagree that the Sentinel application has enhanced the FBI's ability to carry out its mission?	328	498	220	73	24	1143

Question	10 hours or Less	11-20 Hours	21-30 Hours	31-40 Hours	More than 40 Hours Per Week	Total
Please estimate the number of hours per week you used Sentinel during the past 90 days.	355	418	223	111	43	1150

OFFICE OF THE INSPECTOR GENERAL
SENTINEL REPORTS

Report Date	Report Number	Report Title
March 6, 2006	06-14	The Federal Bureau of Investigation's Pre-Acquisition Planning For and Controls Over the Sentinel Case Management System
December 1, 2006	07-03	Sentinel Audit II: Status of the Federal Bureau of Investigation's Case Management System
August 28, 2007	07-40	Sentinel Audit III: Status of the Federal Bureau of Investigation's Case Management System
December 18, 2008	09-05	Sentinel Audit IV: Status of the Federal Bureau of Investigation's Case Management System
November 9, 2009	10-03	Sentinel Audit V: Status of the Federal Bureau of Investigation's Case Management System
March 30, 2010	10-22	Status of the Federal Bureau of Investigation's Implementation of the Sentinel Project
October 19, 2010	11-01	Status of the Federal Bureau of Investigation's Implementation of the Sentinel Project
December 22, 2011	12-08	Status of the Federal Bureau of Investigation's Implementation of the Sentinel Project
September 7, 2012	12-38	Interim Report on the Federal Bureau of Investigation's Implementation of the Sentinel Project

FEDERAL BUREAU OF INVESTIGATION RESPONSE TO THE DRAFT AUDIT REPORT

US Department of Justice

Federal Bureau of Investigation

Washington, D. C. 20535-0001

September 12, 2014

The Honorable Michael E. Horowitz
Inspector General
Office of the Inspector General
U.S. Department of Justice
950 Pennsylvania Avenue, N.W.
Washington, DC 20530

Dear Mr. Horowitz:

The Federal Bureau of Investigation (FBI) appreciates the opportunity to review and respond to your office's report entitled, *Audit of the Status of the Federal Bureau of Investigation's Sentinel Program.*

We are pleased you found, "The majority of FBI employees responding to our survey reported that Sentinel had an overall positive impact on the FBI's operations, making the FBI better able to carry out its mission, and better able to share information." The majority of respondents also noted the "positive impact" on the FBI's efficiency in several areas with the deployment of Sentinel.

We appreciate the collaboration you afforded us on developing the survey questions, recognizing the value added by permitting the FBI to also gather critical user feedback. The FBI remains committed to making Sentinel enhancements to meet mission needs to the best of our ability. In that regard, we concur with the three recommendations made to the FBI and have already taken steps to implement them. Please find enclosed our responses.

Should you have any questions, feel free to contact me. We appreciate the professionalism of your audit staff throughout this matter.

Sincerely,

Jeffrey Johnson
Assistant Director
Information Technology Engineering
Division

The Federal Bureau of Investigation's (FBI) Response to the
Office of the Inspector General's Audit of the Status of the FBI's Sentinel Program
Response to Report Recommendations

Report Recommendation #1: "Evaluate the progress that FBI field offices have made in ensuring that OSTs are fully and effectively performing administrative tasks within Sentinel to optimally reduce the administrative responsibilities of Special Agents."

FBI Response to Recommendation #1: Concur. The FBI will evaluate the progress that FBI field offices have made to ensure that OSTs are fully and effectively performing administrative tasks within Sentinel to optimize the reduction in administrative responsibilities of Special Agents.

Report Recommendation #2: "Solicit user feedback on Sentinel to ensure improvements made to the search function adequately reflect user needs."

FBI Response to Recommendation #2: Concur. The FBI will solicit the feedback of Sentinel users to ensure search function improvements effectively reflect the user needs.

Report Recommendation #3: "Continue to research technological solutions and review business processes and policies to identify ways to reduce the time it takes users to index large unstructured documents."

FBI Response to Recommendation #3: Concur. The FBI will research technological solutions and review business processes and policies to identify ways to reduce the time it takes users to index large unstructured documents.

OFFICE OF THE INSPECTOR GENERAL
ANALYSIS AND SUMMARY OF ACTIONS
NECESSARY TO CLOSE THE REPORT

The Office of the Inspector General (OIG) provided a draft of this audit report to the Federal Bureau of Investigation (FBI). The FBI's response is incorporated in Appendix IV of this final report. The following provides the OIG analysis of the actions necessary to close the report.

Recommendation:

1. **Evaluate the progress that FBI field offices have made in ensuring that Operational Support Technicians (OST) are fully and effectively performing administrative tasks within Sentinel to optimally reduce the administrative responsibilities of Special Agents.**

   Resolved. The FBI concurred with this recommendation. In its response, the FBI stated that it will evaluate the progress that FBI field offices have made in ensuring that OSTs are fully and effectively performing administrative tasks within Sentinel to optimize the reduction in administrative responsibilities of Special Agents.

   This recommendation can be closed when we receive evidence that the FBI has completed evaluations of its field offices' progress to ensure that OSTs are fully and effectively performing administrative tasks within Sentinel. This would include evidence that the administrative responsibilities of Special Agents in FBI field offices have been reduced.

2. **Solicit user feedback on Sentinel to ensure improvements made to the search function adequately reflect user needs.**

   Resolved. The FBI concurred with this recommendation. In its response, the FBI stated that it will solicit user feedback of Sentinel users to ensure search function improvements effectively reflect user needs.

   This recommendation can be closed when we receive evidence that the FBI has continued to solicit user feedback on the search function and that the feedback was used to make improvements that reflect user needs. For each improvement made as a result of this user feedback, the FBI should provide the OIG with a detailed description of the change made and how the search function was improved as a result.

3. Continue to research technological solutions and review business processes and policies to identify ways to reduce the time it takes users to index large unstructured documents.

<u>Resolved.</u> The FBI concurred with this recommendation. In its response, the FBI stated that it will research technological solutions and review business processes and policies to identify ways to reduce the time it takes users to index large unstructured documents.

This recommendation can be closed when we receive documentation showing that the FBI has researched additional technological solutions and reviewed business processes and policies to identify ways to reduce indexing time for large unstructured documents in Sentinel. For each solution implemented and each business process or policy adjustment made, the FBI should provide the OIG with a clear description of the change and the resulting improvements.

www.ingramcontent.com/pod-product-compliance
Lightning Source LLC
Chambersburg PA
CBHW080624290526

45790CB00007B/2908